# BLACKBIRD, BYE BYE

**Moniza Alvi** was born in Pakistan and grew up in Hertfordshire. After working for many years as a secondary school teacher in London, she is now a freelance writer and tutor, and lives in Wymondham, Norfolk. Her latest books – all from Bloodaxe – are *Blackbird, Bye Bye* (2018); her book-length poem, *At the Time of Partition* (2013); *Homesick for the Earth*, her versions of the French poet Jules Supervielle (2011); *Europa* (2008); and *Split World: Poems 1990–2005* (2008), which includes poems from her five previous collections, *The Country at My Shoulder* (1993), *A Bowl of Warm Air* (1996), *Carrying My Wife* (2000), *Souls* (2002) and *How the Stone Found Its Voice* (2005). *The Country at My Shoulder* was shortlisted for the T.S. Eliot and Whitbread poetry prizes, and *Carrying My Wife* was a Poetry Book Society Recommendation. *Europa* and *At the Time of Partition* were selected as Poetry Book Society Choices in 2008 and 2013 respectively and both were shortlisted for the T.S. Eliot Prize. Moniza Alvi received a Cholmondeley Award in 2002. A collection of her poems was published in Italy by Donzelli Editore in their Poesia series in 2014, *Un mondo diviso*, translated by Paola Splendore.

MONIZA ALVI

# Blackbird, Bye Bye

BLOODAXE BOOKS

Copyright © Moniza Alvi 2018

ISBN: 978 1 78037 422 2

First published 2018 by
Bloodaxe Books Ltd,
Eastburn,
South Park,
Hexham,
Northumberland NE46 1BS.

**www.bloodaxebooks.com**
For further information about Bloodaxe titles
please visit our website or write to
the above address for a catalogue.

**ARTS COUNCIL
ENGLAND**

Cover design: Neil Astley & Pamela Robertson-Pearce.

Printed in Great Britain by Bell & Bain Limited, Glasgow, Scotland, on
acid-free paper sourced from mills with FSC chain of custody certification.

# CONTENTS

*Here I go, singin' low*
*Bye, bye blackbird*


FROM 'Bye Bye Blackbird'
(Henderson/Dixon, 1926)

# Motherbird

A big blousy bird in the nest –
   the vee of her beak wide open.

She can only digest little pieces
   broken off the larger offerings.

Sometimes it seems that almost
   every part of Motherbird is sore.

Torn twigs are rough-pricking,
   the floor is mossy and tender.

Rain makes the place uninhabitable.
   The sun tries to dry it.

It's surprising what she fits into a nest
   when I think she alone would fill it.

The boxy, sharp-edged carriage clock
   next to her downy bed belongs

to the grander epoch of Fatherbird.
   It's rain-proof, snow-proof, solid,

its two steely hands telling the truth
   about time and telling a lie.

*I'll come again on Tuesday* I say.
   Her head droops to her breast.

Her eyes close. Motherbird – her stick
   propped against the woven wall.

# Motherbird Can't Fly

Motherbird on my back,
   I cope uncertainly
      with the lift-off. Upstroke

downstroke upstroke
   up up up.
      She is all wingbone

all weighty fragility.
   It's years now since she
      soared into the sky.

*But it's not the same sky!*
   she calls out.
      *Where are we?*

The energy it takes
   to stay up here with her,
      to hover!

*Careful* she cries,
   ever fearful for her life.
      *Look out!*

*Don't fly into the sun.*
   *Don't stall,*
      *don't stop, don't even...*

The wind snatches her voice.
   There's no route,
      no narrative or plot.

The sky has no end
   but we're near the end –
      of somewhere.

## Her Feathers

I envy Motherbird her silky feathers.
   *They're a nuisance* she says,
     *too fine, too fly-away.*
      *They're marvellous* I say –
      but I can't convince her.


     *Motherbird!* I call.
    *Hush!* whisper the feathers.
   *We give little away.*
  *You must place your ear very close*
*to hear our snow-words.*

# The Egg and the Dream

In her mind the egg lies forever
   on its side – its pointed tail-end,
      its malleable shell
         with all the tiny pores to help
         the embryo breathe.

        Such loss of potential
      can't be smoothed over.
    She's right up against it
  with the warmth of her breast,
her incredibly fast-beating heart.

# Motherbird and Her Life So Far

She pecks at the grains and sorts them into piles.

Some she relishes.

Some she doesn't want to think about at all.

A few she doesn't recognise.

So many grains! Such a long life!

Sorting, sorting, shifting to another pile
and back again.

Starting a completely new pile.

All the marked and subtle differences.

The going astray. So much has gone astray that she'll
never get back again.

Or perhaps she will, a little of it.

If she pecks for long enough she might find
the exact grain she's looking for.

Companions?

Now the grains are her companions.

Her eyesight is still quite good.

Something gleams. A jewel!

# Invisible

Her bruises can't be seen
beneath her soft feathers.
     I know they're there.

Once one was exposed –
a mark of violent hues, one shade
     merging into another.

     The roughness of birds.

She would prefer to forget
how she received them.
     I enter into the heart

of the bruise which carries on
bleeding invisibly –
     a single spreading

blue-black-dark-sea stain.
I fly straight into a storm-cloud's
     dreadful purple flowering

     and I take on responsibility

        as if I had caused it.

# Motherbird's Ornament

The glass bird sits

    open-beaked on a glass branch –
        its head lifted towards the light.
            Her guardian, it will not fly away

        until she has flown – then it also
     will surely be gone.
For a glass bird,
            living, dying, transparency –

                nothing is too hard.

## The Coldest Winter

Fatherbird perched on the country's frozen edge.
  England! Bridlington Bay –
    He glanced from side to side
      and the wind blew away each glance.
        The sea with its iron-grey breadth of thought –
          surely the sea would freeze?
            Fatherbird – and a second bird – and a third:
            *It's an opportunity for us.*


        *Then we can return.*
      The sand was a field of snow, strewn
    with the sea's chill gifts. They'd flown
    with the valued cargo of themselves,
  light-weight but strong. Fluffed up their feathers
for warmth. It was their choice.
  The sky was a country of its own. All around them
the seabirds wheeled and cried and laughed.

# When Motherbird Met Fatherbird

and Fatherbird met Motherbird
   so many feathers of the world

were ruffled. It was just after the War –
   and now this war:

*They're from such different countries.*
   *It's unnatural.*

But the clouds parted to let them through.
   The sky rang –

and slowly, deliberately, like a stage-set
   a whole landscape slid into place.

With certainty – and uncertainty
   Motherbird and Fatherbird flew off.

Flew back. And settled.
   They didn't just drift like leaves.

*This is our home now* they said –
   stretching the world at its seams.

## Golden Bird

*Goodbye* she cried out, *goodbye*.

She didn't know for how long.

Her feathers were corn-gold, sun-gold, rose-gold
the year she flew East
and further East, against all advice,
bravely betrothed,
her first long-distance flight.

The sky deepened to sapphire.

At first she hardly missed England at all.
And then? With motherhood the darkness fell.
She was more wingbeats away from home
than there were waves in the sea.

What could they do, but leave?

*Goodbye* they both said. *Goodbye*.

# Motherbird Sings

Though she no longer soars
　　to France or Spain
　　　　she carries in her bones

the memory of flight
　　the long enchantment of it.
　　Haltingly she sings

in those other languages –
　　French is her sun
　　　　Spanish, her moon.

She practises each note.
　　A tentative joy
　　　　these flights of song –

each phrase
　　a little succulence
　　　　in her head, her throat.

# A Photo of Fatherbird

We don't speak of him very much
　　though in his frame he sings and sings:
　　　*Here I am! Here I am!*
　　He perches just above life
　　　handsome, brown-feathered
　　　　a migrant –
　　　　　so many birds rolled into one.


　　　We're shaken – the treetop
　　　　is swaying in a gale.
　　Fatherbird stabs and stabs
　　　at the living world
　　and he's almost broken through.
　　*Welcome* we say to him. *Welcome back.*
*I am ever-present* he sings.
　　　　　*I can't come back.*

# The Afterlife of Fatherbird

# 1

Now that he's dead Fatherbird walks even more unsteadily
flies even more erratically –
   and as he walks he tries to pluck words out of the air

as if he's plucking feathers.
   All the words float off, they're made of such a light substance.
   They don't want to stick to him any more.

I wouldn't think he'd need words now, but he does.
   Motherbird has so many and can't give him any of them –
   it was the same in the last of his living years.

# 2

Now that he's dead I'm waiting for Fatherbird to visit me
   in a dream.
   Months and years have passed.

Perhaps he's waiting too – for the right moment.
   Perhaps he doesn't know that this is possible for him.
   Or it could be that he has more pressing things to do.

Perhaps he's enjoying the soft ripeness of a mango
   the juice running down his front?
   It may be a question of patience.

Fatherbird, there's a space for you, should you wish to visit –
   dreams are such large
                    hospitable places.

**3**

Now that he's dead, Fatherbird flies back and further back
    racing past the dementia years
        not perching on a single traumatic moment –

until there he is! Youthful, bold and in full voice
    lively in debate.
    He nestles against this point in time, listens

to his young and popular self, gathers together
    the words he had then, picking them up
        singly and examining them, all the words

he'd been unable to hoard to get him through
    the lean times. These words for everything, they shine
    like small stones underwater! Served him well

                        when they could be found at all.


**4**

*It's impossible to grow old with dignity* you said.
    Dignity. Now you're dead you're regaining it bit by bit.
    I'm so relieved it's reattaching itself to you.

You raise your head which had fallen to your breast
    preen your thin, bedraggled feathers and they respond
        sharpen your curved beak on a rock.

You practise speaking. You take more certain steps.
    The left, the right
                        your eyes recover their intelligence.

**5**

Now that you're dead, I think your first country
   the one you half-bestowed on me, has almost gone –
     slipping away like the striped tail-end of something.

I hadn't thought a country could die in this way, its edges
   blurring, its heat not quite as strong.
     I swivel my head, imagine you opening your wings –
                               and it's there.


**6**

Fatherbird, now that you're dead you seem more alive
   than when you were truly alive.
     Then you could hardly speak, let alone sing.

Now it's as if you've been shaken by a hurricane.
   Even your soul is in better shape.
     You look much younger, almost in your prime.

Yet you look sad. Perhaps you're missing us...
   Perhaps you have regrets...
     But Fatherbird
              even the past has passed.

     *Ah* you say, *all is present.*
                 *Absent and present.*

# 7

You knew (perhaps still know) so much about flight –
  the long-haul, the slow-looping against
    the wind and into the sun, the disentangling.

When to halt and where to settle, when to carry on
  and who to choose for company.
    At one with your soul, you flew beneath

between and over, East-West, West-East, carved a way
  into the unfamiliar, made your own weather –
    captain of the flying club for years

      until swiftly, acutely, you flew one way

        and the world the other.


# 8

You did revisit me, just once.
  I turned the corner and there you were –
    I hadn't seen you land.

Clearly you must have had the urge to return –
  to see and to be seen.
    You were palpably you, Fatherbird

not transparent at all. Still and quiet
  and soaked
    in that beautiful aura of life.

**9**

In seconds you flew away, just vanished –
    and resolutely
                 kept on being dead.


**10**

And there you still are
    moments after you've died, lying awkwardly
        on your side, the wind parting your feathers

                    as if you were still alive.


**11**

*I'm a simple soul!* You used to claim
    ignoring our looks of disbelief.
        Fatherbird, I wonder if, yourself intact

      you've reached a place of true simplicity?

## 12

You had a talent for friendship, were drawn to
    other migrants, all of you holding
        the fine wavering thread between here and there.

And now I picture you glancing around for a soul-mate
    and finding him.
        It would be all geniality, the drinking and teasing

the two of you with still so much to say about
    East and West and the flying between –

                                    and this other strange passage.


## 13

Now that you're dead, Fatherbird, I hesitate to bring you
    news of the world – but what else is our world made of
        and where else is there for your thoughts to fly?

        Maybe you know the worst already –
                                    you bow your head.

Don't think about this now.
    You don't need to – I can bring you happier news
        of little things. It's been a hot week, we're active

in the evenings. The rose is blooming, the rambling one
    your favourite, milky white with a yellow heart.
        So many flower-heads! We want it to bloom forever.

        *Bring me news!* you cry.
                        *More news of the world!*

## 14

At last you've surprised me, swooping into a dream,
    as robust as any bird, in the full brilliance
        of your afterlife, radiating that sense of yourself.

You stayed, or I allowed you to stay
    for just a few moments.
        *Ah, Moniza!* you called out with enthusiasm

        just as you often did –

                that slight emphasis on the 'z'.


## 15

A young bird was dying, Fatherbird, and she wanted
    everyone to look into one of her eyes, as if
        in a single eye there was something terrible to see.

One by one all of those gathered around gazed
    with their own clear eyes.
        I alone couldn't look into the young bird's eye.

*Is she going to die?* I asked. *Oh yes* was everyone's reply.
*You must look!* she said.
        Her feathered head touched mine.

    With the wisdom of the dead
                can you tell me, Fatherbird

        what was in her eye?

## 16

Fatherbird, who'd have imagined for you an exile
   this complete? Once again you rowed the boat
     of yourself, exchanging one country for another.

      It was rarely easy. You rowed and rowed.
                      It was winter.

# Chinese Story

I remember it, and don't remember it:

the wooden birdcages, the birdcatcher who took
the bright birds backwards and forwards
to the market in a handcart. They were so alive
and sweet-singing in their cages.

Then something happened –
disappointing that I can't recall exactly what.
There must have been conflict, an argument
and I'm sure a second birdman was involved.

At some point the birds were probably freed
to encircle the heads of the birdcatchers
in a yellow, white and red conflagration.
The tale was sunny and how could it have been

so full of light if they were never freed –
but who knows? It wasn't a celebrated story
like 'The Emperor and the Nightingale'
and I may never trace it, but it still flickers,

the colours of the birds accented by distance.
I can see the town's network of bleached lanes,
the birdcatchers' pointed straw hats
and the thin black tendrils of their moustaches.

I know that little needs to happen in a story
as long as it resonates. And this one does –
its intimation of China.
The birds were the story's active soul,

the cages almost as lovely as they were –
tiered and decorative, like crowded palaces.
As for the people, there were just so many
as could comfortably fit inside a story.

*Three poems inspired by the paintings of Remedios Varo*

## A Portrait of the World

So this is the world
with its startled brown eyes
and curved shoulders,
the vermilion and black
of its seas and continents.

But have I understood the look?
The pupils are sharp, tiny.
One eye-socket extends into a wing
and the other, to a fish's tail.

The muscular swish of the tail!
The proud, strong arc of the wing!

The world's forehead rises
into a pointed hat
of rugged mountain.
Its hair is scarlet,
the chin is ringed by a fiery beard.

I'm haunted by the world's shoulders,
its melancholic mouth,
the lit vulnerability of its face
which, above an inferno

holds fins and feathers
in balance,
so that despite it all –
the carnage, the onslaught
of the centuries –

a gold-green fish swims,
a pale bird flies.

# Creating the Birds

I am the owl-artist, delineating each feather
my eyes half-closed, deep in the hollows

of my mask-like face.
It's hard to tell where my woman self

begins and the owl ends –
tawny feathers cover most of me,

but I've a woman's bare hands and feet.
You could say I'm an alchemist

though I've only a few transmuting devices –
the complex work goes on within.

I apply the finishing brushstrokes to a tail
and at once the bird lifts off from the paper

and rises to the arched window.
A few I tame with crumbs, try to keep.

They're lovelier than I am, more complete.
I'm in my vaulted studio all night.

I don't know where they come from.
A kind of sleep? And before that?

And before that?

# Allegory of Winter

*You've imprisoned us.*

Dear birds,
I promise you won't die.
You won't starve.
I'm protecting you
from winter's assault.

*We don't always starve*
*in the cold months.*

You look so spring-like
in your transparent
diamond casings.
How exquisite you all are,
so bright and various,
each of you an artist.
Each of you poised
on the brink of flight.

*We're sealed off,*
*can only glimpse each other.*
*The enormous snowflakes*
*are blue with cold,*
*the sky is grey-indigo.*
*The branchless trees*
*have deep whorls*
*and the gashing spines*
*of giant brown cacti.*
*They bend towards us like humans.*
*Release us, we beg you*
*into actual spring.*

I can't quite hear you.

*We're muffled*
*beyond endurance.*

I too despair that beauty
should be so confined.
Hold your breath.
Forgive me
for taking you by surprise.
It's winter – a savage time.
Can you bear it?

# The Empty Nest

The sun slips through.
The bowl is warmed.
You can't quite call it empty
when there's air in it
and still more air.

Wedged in a fork of the apple tree
it's in no danger of falling.
It looks so small and humble,
a simple room, though actually
it's a masterwork –

refined, with a velvety floor.
The wind blows unevenly
and once we heard it howl:
*They've gone!*
No one saw them leave

asked them how they fared
or where they were heading.
We suppose their wings
were streaked with enthusiasm.
Is there really such a thing

as a new life?
After all, we've each
been allocated just one.
But then sometimes we're sure
that a different version

has shaken us up and claimed us.
What can we drop in here –
a strip of foil, a piece of shell?
Invited, uninvited
something will move in.

# A Soft White Feather Lying on the Grass

What does the feather say to the grass?
Well, nothing at all.
And yet there is a conversation –
filament to blade, blade to filament.
The feather gives the impression
of being complete in itself,
never a part of something
never a fully-functioning part of a bird.
The blades clearly need each other
just as they require the feather
to bring them into brilliance.
Nothing is just white or green
or completely alone.
Is this true, or partly true?
The circumstance of the feather
touches the circumstance of the grass.

Both wait.

The grass is the more patient.

# November Trees

Alders hold up their nests
close to the winter sky
        like lamps on long stems –
this is what the trees do
for the birds: the rooks
and their young.
I study the alders' tall,
slim frames supporting
the stick nests –
it seems at this dark time,
when so much has failed
and the country of my birth
becomes ever more unsafe,
that the trees are generous
to the birds
        and the busy,
instinctive act of nest-building
is one of perfect trust –

# Stories

## *Distress*

a leaf is hopping
it lifts     its frail head
knocks at a stone
shakes slightly     judders
and sways     falls back
tries to raise itself
its single leaf-wing
still breathes     dry
hop-hopping
sipping at gravel

## *No loading*

a flock of them     skitters     whirls up
maddened     desperate to keep together
a few not swept up     striving     to join the others
almost catching up     tossed aside     mid-flight
as the great crowd     crosses     the double yellow lines
lands on     NO LOADING     then nearly all of them
swept away     to spin just above     the concourse
and arrive again on     NO LOADING

## With abandon

Bowling along    spiralling    it suddenly
flutters down    lands flat on its back
and encircling it    at different heights
the tall grasses are perpetually
sumptuously    agitated

# The Callers

They came to call
on us
a group of them
they were persistent
some had no beaks
just a rough-looking
raised part
where the hard lips
had been
we had no door
to shut against them
we knew
they knew this
they had no words
not a single word

# The Vanishing Point

*We'll fly in tandem* Death said
and she touched her wingtip to mine.

*Trust me, you'll not fear the winter.*
*It's growing quiet now. Quiet as an egg.*

I waited for her in the reeds –
just at the edge of the shallow pool.

She beat her wings like the sea.

*You can sing.*
*Sing as loudly as you like.*

*You're used to soaring*
*out of sight, I know.*

*We're birds*
*of a feather, absolutely all of us.*

*Very soon we'll rest.*
*And then, if you like, we can play –*

*breast to breast, wing to wing.*
*It will be pleasant enough.*

## Being Alive

*(after Jules Supervielle)*


All because I stepped
on the heart of night
I find myself caught
in the snare of the stars.

I know nothing of the peace
that comes to humankind,
even my sleep
is wolfed down by the sky.

In their utter nakedness
my days are crucified,
the forest birds iced-up
in the summer air.

*Ah! You're dropping, dropping from the trees.*

# To the Birds

*(after Jules Supervielle)*


Cardinals, rollers, calandrias and tanagers,
living flames, birds torn from the sun,
drive away, away and away the cruel
inertia which has seized my spirits.

Bramblings, chaffinches, is it you
who'll come and surprise with glowing feathers
this torpor which has taken such a hold
and gives up on each day without tasting it?

Free, I want at last to overcome this slackness,
to see the sky mad with joy beneath an explosion
of swallows, crying of a thousand other horizons,
to live at ease at last in my brain's gentleness.

If need be, to shake off this hardened sadness,
I'll hail, on the threshold of hidden forests,
a haphazard flock of red and green parrots
to crack open my soul in sparks of light.

# Birds and Naturalists

*(after Saint-John Perse)*


The first naturalists with their careful, reverential language
examined our wings closely (the shaft, barbs and vane
of our feathers, our primaries and secondaries, large
motor pinions and all the striping and freckling
of our adult plumage) and they were able to venture closer
to our bodies themselves, called them our topography
as if we were minute pieces of land, showed us
for our true double selves, of the air and of the earth,
tiny satellites of the circling planet.

They studied our light architecture,
made for the take-off and duration of flight,
our breasts fashioned like boats, the strong-room
of our hearts, entered only by the arterial flow, secret
caging for the delicacy of our muscles and ligaments.
They admired our winged, urn-shaped bodies,
their subtlety and passion, marvelled at our systems,
the spaces and crevices for quick oxidation, branching,
copying veins connected to our backbones and phalanges.

With our hollow bones and air sacs carrying us
more lightly than straw to the splendour of full flight,
we defied all that was known of aerodynamics.
The student or too curious child, having dissected
one of us won't be able to forget how nautical we are,
how naturally we copy the ships, ribcage like a hull,
bony mass – the fo'c'sle, breastbone – the spar,
our shoulder blades – rowlocks where the oars
of our wings engage, pelvic girdle – the stern...

## At the Frontier

*(after Saint-John Perse)*


We're spears raised at the frontier of the human world!
With our strong, calm wings, our eyes washed clear
we forge ahead, enjoying our liberty across the seas,
soaring over the ports and bazaars of the Levant...
We make long pilgrimages, crusaders beneath
the cross of our wings. Could any well-blessed
sea-route show such a mass of sails?

We go where all birds go, together with
all the beings that travel the earth's surface,
drifting on the flux of time towards the same fate,
the great swell where everything heads,
the heavenly bodies on their circuit, the force of life
which stirs in the depths of a May night.
We fly further than we'd ever imagined
and then we disappear, leaving to human beings
the ocean of all that is free – and far from free.

Unaware of our own shadows, what we know
of death is only the eternal
heard in the surge of distant waves.
The space we cross is a single human thought.
Humans! We leave them, altering them forever.

We're rock-still, mute, our wings tensed
then silently we wheel high in the vastness
of the human night. But we return at dawn
as strangers, clothed in the tar and frost
of the earth's first morning
and in our cleansed freshness we guard
for humankind something of creation's dream.

# The Bird and the Artist

*(after Saint-John Perse)*


Most lordly of all the hunters and fishers
who frequent the sky, I swoop down on my prey
from a great height, swapping in a sliver of time
the most distant vision for intimate inspection.
Delicate muscles control, this way,
that way, the crystalline curve of my pupils.
Outspread like a Winged Victory, I'm consumed
in the sheer force of my own descent,
mingling in a single flame both sail and sword.
Then, all soul and torn soul, I plunge
trembling like a knife, to merge with my prize.

I'm the lightning flash of the artist, predator
and prey, piercing, direct, then achieving my goal
with a sideways or, better still, a circling motion.
And so I perform my long, determined search.
My reward? I'm at peace with my guest.
This is the shared secret of artist and bird!
Stopped in flight, I'm hurled down
on the lithographer's plate to live
in a mutating cycle: metamorphosis,
shifts of key, a series of birdshapes
leading to a full revelation.

At last it will be uncovered,
the clarity of the deepest mystery –
the one self under so many.

# A Long Reign

The King of the Birds
is dead.
His feathers have been rearranged,

smoothed down, his wings folded.
He looks almost as good as new –
plumper, like a stuffed bird

and with a satin sheen.
We're perched on the sides
of his wooden box, peering in,

terrified of falling down
or brushing against him
feather to feather.

He's scarlet and gold –
impressive lying in state.
It's the not-him

that is so frightening,
that buzzes and outlines him
and swells, almost filling

what was once his kingdom.
Semi-confident, unencumbered
by his difficult, demonstrative

rule, singly, and in pairs
we patrol the woods.

We're a republic now.

# Blood Feathers

The rings of your eyes: the outer the inner
    the perfect dreaming circles

Midday the light
    gilded your feathers all but one

Elegant blue/black bird
    shadowy larger than you were

Galeforce bird buffeted here
    never completely at home

Our feathers were torn out stricken
    you were wrong we were all wrong

Your generous your severe self
    the one turning from the other

We were so small pressing ourselves
    tight against the wall of the nest

We stood with you on a remote branch
    the leaves shivered

We learned to fly quietly and to wait
    until the colossal storm clouds passed

Under our blood feathers
    nothing ever quite subsided

We stored in our mild breasts a rage
    that only the elements understood

Somehow the sun still did come out
    loud and clear and smaller suns too

In all weather we did what we could
    contented ourselves with veering

(Blood feathers, also called pin feathers, are new feathers that
are starting to grow.)

# No Comfort

'I,' said the dove
'I mourn my love'.

('Who killed Cock Robin?')


The dove pines
in her cramped corner.
Chief comforter,

I offer her some seed-cake.
Caraway seeds, Persian cumin –
she pecks them all out.

They're small and ribbed
and warmly aromatic
but they don't help.

We gathered around him,
before and after –
though none of us,

not even the fly
saw him die.

# The Tree

It was a tree in two halves –

one half a mango
and the other an oak.

You were perched
somewhere in the middle

though in your last months
you favoured the mango.

It took you such a long time to fall,
gripping and gripping the branch.

You must have landed with a thud.
Perhaps you even heard it.

Sad departure – or the relief of arrival.

The day you dropped
from the tree like a fruit.

# Fatherbird's Despair

In a 'home' far from home, and blindfold now,

he hunts around for lost trinkets – Indian gold.

# The Nest They Made

They made ours differently.
Lined it with scraps from here – and there,
pieces of knotted Bokhara rugs and threads
from gauzy Indian scarves. Pressed
tiny mirrors into bright straw.

Some weeks they couldn't afford
to pay the rent. We hid ourselves
as best we could.
Our nest was high up, glittery.
They built and built.

# Dark Bird

Now that you and almost all
your friends have gone
I'll say that none of you
was solidly black, but speckled,
streaked, banded –
different on different days.

You were a parent
with patterned under-wings
and a single orange feather
like a little flame
that keeps on burning
so I can still

make you out – dark bird
against the dark.

# What I hear now is tuneless

a stammer a slight
trembling a wavering
silver note or two
behind a screen

and what else?
and whether? not that
not entirely anything
of earth or sky

cast on the air
and fished for
a frost-bitten phrase
chill diminuendo

a hanging casual
post-it note
or more desperate
does birdsong freeze?

and still an under-
tone there it is
again and almost
too much

# The Mirror

*(after Jules Supervielle)*

Give her a mirror halfway across the road,
she'll see life in it, slipping through her hands,
a glittering star like an irregular heart
which sometimes beats too fast, or beats too faintly.

When her favourite birds fly close
she'll look at them without recognition
and terror-struck, she'll try to glimpse her face –
the mirror will be speechless, silent forever.

# Less, much less

He hardly spoke any words
only two –
or you could call it one

the last thing
he said
was bye-bye

flight-feathers
veined and hairlike
with interlocking barbules

of sound
the bye-bye trapped
a breath of air

the two linked words
drifted out
on a calm lake

that lay there
with a single purpose –
to receive final words

and allow them
to drift on its surface
out and further out

on the lake of thought
and composure
encircled by mountains

the simple phrase
soared upwards
to the highest peak

where it would be planted
like a flag
would eventually be enshrined

each identical word carefully
balanced either side
of the invisible join –

like baby talk
he put equal emphasis
on each word

his   face was pinched
and his bird beak
very prominent

there have never been
two joined words
with so much space around them

pack up all my cares and woes
light the light
I'll arrive    late tonight

blackbird    bye bye

bye

# ACKNOWLEDGEMENTS

Thanks are due to the editors of the following publications in which some of these poems first appeared: *A Restricted View from Under the Hedge*, *Artemis*, *F(r)iction* (USA), *Himal* (South Asian), *Long Poem Magazine*, *Ploughshares* (USA), *Poetry* (USA), *Poetry London*, *The Saint Ann's Review* (USA), *The London Magazine*, *The Poetry Review*, and *The Scores*.

The poem 'Invisible' was commissioned for *The Caught Habits of Language*, edited by Rachael Boast, Andy Ching and Nathan Hamilton (Donut Press, 2018), an anthology celebrating the centenary of W.S. Graham.

I would like to thank all those who gave invaluable assistance with this collection, including the members of the the National Theatre group, and Mara Bergman, Jane Duran and Heidi Williamson. Particular thanks to Susan Wicks who read and commented on the manuscript.

For the versions of Saint-John Perse, I'm indebted to the more literal *Birds* by Saint-John Perse: a version by Derek Mahon (The Gallery Press, 2002).

The poem 'The Empty Nest' is dedicated to Diane DeBell.